Tomorrow

Don Schaeffer

Cyberwit.net
HIG 45 Kaushambi Kunj, Kalindipuram
Allahabad - 211011 (U.P.) India
http://www.cyberwit.net
Tel: +(91) 9415091004
E-mail: info@cyberwit.net

Printed at Repro India Limited.

This book is dedicated to my Granddaughter, Hannah Zoe, who had her special Bat Mitzvah in May, 2021, a pandemic year.

I begin with four poems I wrote in the first 6 months of her life. Best of good fortune, Hannah Zoe.

Contents

On Being Rejected by a Baby

When they are
eight months old
they temporarily attain
the ability to look
directly into your
internal record
of evil and good
They accept you
and reject you as if
they were standing
behind the desk
of Puritan heaven.
Oh tiny Hannah
why did you spurn me
and pass your
darkened face my way?
I worry that
the neighbor woman
who brings about your smile
will record a
bigger deeper heart
than I.

The Beatitude of Six Months Hannah

When the baby is well fed
she smiles not with well being
but with beneficence,

deep into my face as if promising
a special gift, wishing honor and fortune.
She, princess of prophecy, savior of the world,
reincarnation of Düsum Khyenpa, knower of three times,

regards me with kindness,
guards me within her
protective shield,
knows my thoughts
and judges me charitably.

I leave her and my face
shines golden with her blessing.
I stand out, singular in a crowd ,
fitted into the cross word
puzzle of her mind.
And when her face
curls into a cry, it vanishes.

Hannah the Face Prophet

Your parents court you
and so does your aunt,
not serious rivals of course.
Your grandfather courts you too.
All of us want

a portion of your smile.
You are just learning
how to make a smile, not
a simple act of construction
it turns out. But the smile
you bear fulfills prayers.

Oh Hannah whose smile is sought,
I am among those who
sit at your feet
mesmerized by hope I can
bring about the lighting of those lips.

You will say, "yes." You will approve.
But what do you give me
when I win your smile?
You just say "yes."
There will be no gift.

Hannah and the Light Machine

She learns
to create
with her eyes.
While the tears
are about to grow.

I can walk her
astraddle my arm
under the ceiling lamp
and her eyes will fill with stars.

So I bought her
a color maker
that splashes circles
on the walls

and she will own them
toying with sight
even as the tears
recede.

Hannah and the Light Machine
Don Schaeffer l.08

January 09, 2008

Tomorrow

I'm sure you will suspect something not right. I will tell you. This is not about the usual tomorrow. It's about alternatives. It's about life no longer being as I know it. It's about what replacement possibilities are there. What hints may lay in the alternative worlds that surround me every day and every minute? Alternatives may lay dormant even in my own mind. What could experience be in the alternative? Does that count for me? As we age, we don't look at tomorrow in the same way.

In the Morning

Bluebirds would trill
under the floral sunshine.
The sweet air spread
like a roadway through time,
missing all the unlucky spots.

Then just today
the birds stopped singing.
The air closed.
It was still air and sweet
but the future went out of it.

My Western Wall

My walls are a lattice of impressions,
an un-narratable story,

from the copied small portrait
of children born of a far away daughter,
half-erased with white crayon

to the fleeting glimpse of a poorly maintained stop sign
and the dream of a bullfight.

Alex, in her white dress
is glaring into a display screen
in the booth for having your say,
the image poorly rendered,
scribbled and pressed to the bare wall with tape.

A vision of a spider's orb made into a torch
by the sun amid the green and black
of Long Island's trees,
an over-processed photograph rendered in pastel.

The stark prairie earth abstracted
under the fluid skies.

I have lived amid many walls
which are quickly covered with the inside of my eyes.

Not Packing Just Thinking

Tomorrow may not
be around here.
We may have shared
a slot of time, a joy.

But tomorrow may not
be the same. I may
awake and
not remember you.

I may not awake.
A stranger,
hardly a memory,
I have stopped asking,

have travelled
between worlds and
have visions of what it
may be like if it is anything.
It may not be around here.

Microscopy

When I make the first cut
it looks like I'm slicing a grapefruit.
I rip into the flesh and the water flows
all over the glass. Then I begin
scraping the bubbly skin
which splits into shards on the puddle surface.
I want to make the gelatin solid,
take away most of its natural character
and claim it is something else,
making it dry and flat.
Then I look into it's insides
pretending it's the surface
of an alien planet and I've
travelled deep and long to reach it.

10 AM

Today I kidnapped
a little flower,
a bit of purple,
glowing in the grim
jungle of early Spring slivers.
I didn't treat her gently.
I ripped off the petals
and sliced the stem,
glaring under the
instruments that helped me
see the flesh torn and the
life syrup oozing from the wounds.
I sought secrets
in the folds of those skirts.
I spread it out on a glass
and invited my friends to see.
Inside the flesh were
long-lost cities with
walls made of transparent jade,
trails through forests festooned with fruit.

Evolution

We don't know
if the cells that
swam in the primal pool
knew anything but
if they were alive they
certainly had intentions.
Life is driven and selfish.

We don't know when
at first they decided
to come together,
making pretty circles
but it became a habit
until the ones on
the inner track began
to look different.

We don't know when
the choices slipped their genes
and choice was stolen.
The wills of creatures
that were free became
a formulation of birth.

They spoke
the language of chemistry
from the first and still do,
moving from team to organism.
Who has the power to rule
these giants of a billion chemical voices?

Life in Jerusalem

I wish I lived
in a world of
beautiful happenstance,
like them.

.

When they acted on truth,
released the truth
pushing it through
the tough lining of fear,
longings ached, but there were
always graceful remedies.

.

There might have been a time
when hope was strong enough
for that. Hope doesn't age well.

The Machine Part

It's been happening lately.
I'm discovering a technology
of what makes me tick and applying
these learned principles as if I
were a machine. The poetry knew these rules
but I have just learned them.

There are strange things that excite
and frighten me, that pass like air
when they are finished. These are not real,
come from the hell of whirling memory.

But now I know to use them unashamedly.
There are levers in my heart that can be
flipped with mental fingers, things that
remain secret in life and reverberate with
embarrassment that could last beyond death.

Insect in the Tub

There was a small beetle
in the tub when
I went to take a shower.
This time I didn't feel like
drowning it or squashing it
as I ordinarily might to
excise my fear.

.

I wrapped the insect in
paper and, naked, stepped
out of the tub into the
empty hallways, opened the door
and tossed it onto the porch.
When I returned to the tub I
confronted my naked body in
in the full-length mirror on the door.
I hadn't met this man eye-to-eye
for maybe 20 years. Hello I said,
not bad for your age.

Essence

You want to know where your essence is?
A small cyst below your right nipple
holds a milky stuff
with a fragrance you will recognize,
not pleasant, but familiar
like memory, like infancy,
and what your cat uses
to know you are home.

Do you remember
what it was like
to be a smelling creature?
Think back to when
the light was poor and
there was only time.
You secreted your name.

Down in the darkness
where you don't want to go,
the tribes were mounting
flags of protein. You
could count the packets
to know who was there,
body close, reassured.

Quantum Mechanics

These doctors know they have a problem.
The tiny wave-thing appears in two
places at the same time.
So there must be two universes
and we, for an instant, get to live in both.

.

Damn the mathematics that it should lead us
to share such strange notions;
and what happens when the time is up?
Well we have converted belief into knowledge.

.

Another scientist states a clean viewpoint
on the issue saying,
"It's simply the best we can do."

Decor

Those pictures
which I made
stopped moving long ago.
Now they just remind me.
The walls I stacked
with thoughts have become
recollections, no longer brave,
no longer hopeful.
I have tried to make eyes dance
and they have retired.

I'm surprised

how much of my time I spend crying.
Its all the time

I spend with ghosts.
Dark shadows making holes in the light,

all of the farewells
and the never agains

pull on the levers
of my pumps,

behind the scenes,
no one looking.

How Well Did I Love?

Here I thought
I loved so well.
Well, I can still
see your face.
I remember the feel of you.
I remember how love drove
the puzzlement of rage.

How well did I really do love?
I don't long for you.
My life has reverted into habit.
I wouldn't welcome your ghost.

Fading Civilization

The new person
has a lonely spirit,
close to the loss of speech.

I feel her unfamiliarity
every time she tries
to respond to my good morning.

Mark Honigncamo

He was an artist in an
unusual sense. He documented
a pathology of daily dreaming,
acted out with comic book Barbie dolls
recorded in photographs.
.

They made the pictures the size of
walls, for the gallery.
He told stories of a perversion with guns
and Nazis in a small New York town.
The solitude of the artist,
.

The loss in his vivid dreaming,
was punctuated with anxious women
who tried to understand him,
without giving themselves away.
There were lots of tears
and tender statements of concern.

The First Four Days of Creation

On day one
the aliens invented time
and the worm could exist in it's blindness.

On the second day they made light
and invented the idea of eyes.
Then they grabbed the light with their mind-hands
and spread it out so things could appear.

They invented atoms and learned the tricks
of locks and keys so life could be created and link and speak.
Cells could make themselves known and join together.

On day four, they invented history.

I Put Away My Tools

Mischievously,
she remembers how she needs
the little tenderness
that she forgot all night
just as I start to write,

.

I grant her tiny
black and white wish,
a healing purr
which adds months to her life,

.

the small bit,
the hint of a gift.

The Dread

I saw a movie about a war.
They kept the vision real,
and it was daytime in Spring
when true death was in the air.
There was fear,
on solid ground,
on top of the ordinary earth.
We cried
but there was no dread.
The dread came
later in the dark,
in abandonment by friends
and half confessed secrets
and lies.

Life Doesn't Need Your Input

Don't choose
the choices can
pick you or not.

.

The criteria are
vague and inscrutable.
Everyone picks life,

.

a natural commandment,
The heat of your choosing
issues out into the cold.

.

Anyway the choices
are already made, it's now
sentiment only.

A Scene from Firebird

They gang up on him
when he tries to enter through the gate.
It is the rigidity of folk tales.
Moving like insects,
spines maybe severed from brains,
their movement repetitiously tight,
in a motion prison without escape.
That is what frightens
all the tender ones,
motion slavery, arms in eternal quiver,
faces taken away,
twisted behind them,
and strange formations grown on their backs.
They can only gesticulate,
nothing to do with death,
they paralyze.

One Morning

I awoke one morning
and the great people had already been decided.
Sorry I didn't make the cut.
There are no more lifetimes to try.
And I will never stop wondering.

First Thing

I wake to small things,
gratefully, surrounded
by what I touch and smooth with my fingers.

My private past rushes
into my vision like the
cold burst of a pond through a broken dam.

I know that grander things are coming.
The future will also burst and flood.
I will lock my eyes on it at some waking.

Little Bedtime Prayer

God, I said,

if I feel so lost
when I am in my bed, how will it be when
I am at the precipice where there are no roads?

Why do I just feel so much safer, God, when
I am protecting someone else?

Dear God,
is it valid to feel
danger when I am at the place where fear
no longer works?

COVID Shot One

Behaving all during the slow passage
through what will yet be something historic,
through the solemn and respectful stations,
I felt pride and comfort and I behaved myself.

I moved in respectful silence as they
gently took my ignorance away,
as I felt them ordering my steps
and locking them into time.

We all agreed, the thousands
sprawled around the floor.
We felt the grandeur that left us silent.

Primitive Living

Space is always there
even without eyes.
On a dim day
in a curtain of blue
time moves like a ribbon.
Change is life
not lost on you
rising and falling
saying things in a
language of speed and grit,
reaching into the heights.
You know the division
into cells of experience
embodied in time,
apart and together,
sound and breath.

The Formula for Good Opera

Hope is good.
Hope sells tickets.
The best selling operas
offer hope just before death.
It's a heart twister
and the audience eats it up.

It takes them while they're young
when hope has the biggest draw
then plays on early demise
the audience gets to watch
hope fading in those lovely eyes,
delicious.

All they want is a
time and place,
a calm, a breath, a sigh
together with a reliable love.
It's just a humble wish
but you have to be young to wish it.

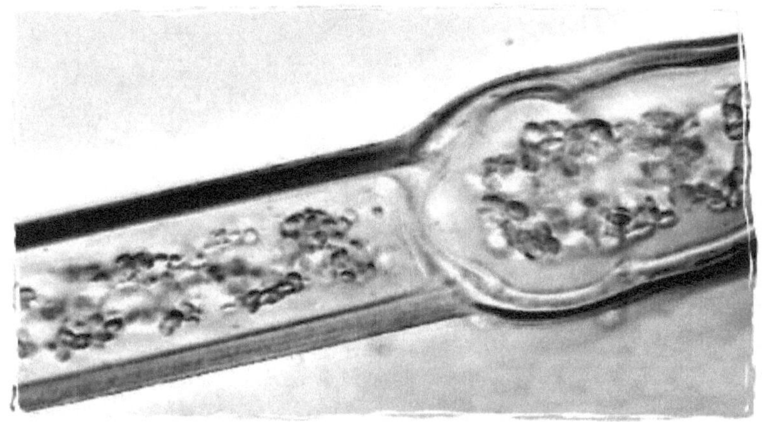

The Final Creation

It was the eighth day and the world was built.
God had rested from his labors.

There was still no elegance.
And God said I will make it.

God plunged his fingers into the eyes
of the creatures and corrupted them,

making a hunger.
And so was elegance born.

The Switchboard

We use a well developed code
the genes have long known how to duplicate.
Now they are all locked in.

The noise here is deafening
but we now have the personnel
to handle it.

I hate to use
such coarse words to refer
to our work here. It's a kind of joke with us.

The point is we receive each message
and respond in a language
they are calling "accident."

Our Fellows in the Swamp

water
contained only by a spell
that intensifies the surface films,
whatever the water does, they do
separation so thin,
they live softly.
barely keep themselves
from bursting.

Ancestors in the Dark Water

Why should we envy them?
We can do what they do.
They live for perspiration.
Excreting is how they talk,
sending messages of body products,
listening for echoes with their skins.

Scienc Lesson

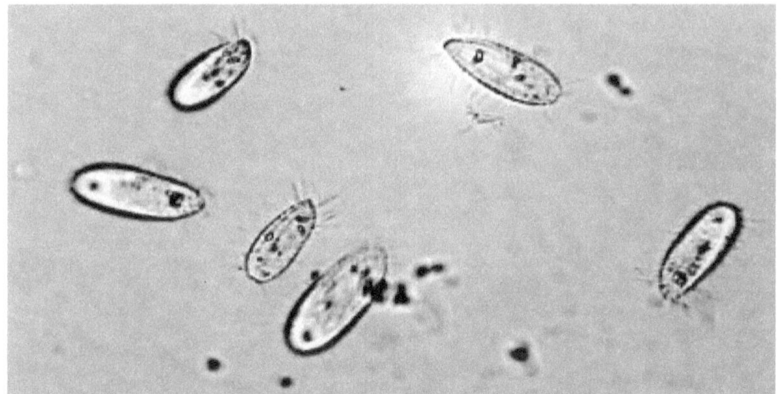

The Failure of Parsimony

For those who live by simple principles,
life should begin with loneliness,
singularity is parsimony when you can manage it.
But in the dimness of far away
on the other planets
that co-occur in this world
the creatures gather and organize.
They speak chemical languages,
the words drawing them together.